A Passing Breeze

A Passing Breeze

Poems by Dale G. Dunn

A Passing Breeze
Copyright 2019 by Dale G. Dunn

Dale G. Dunn
dgddvm@gmail.com

ISBN: 978-0-578-61195-2

Printed in the United States of America

First Printing, 2019

Editing: Tell Tell Poetry | www.telltellpoetry.com
Design: Cover&Layout | www.coverandlayout.com

For my family and friends,
constant sources of inspiration.

A Passing Breeze

Contents

I leave these words to
read someday when they are long
forgotten and laugh.

Spring: Prudence

Cloud Shadows

The sun blinks.

Waves of inky shadows
suffuse parchment fields.

Crocus

The first to rise,
she wiped her eyes.
The clearing snow awoke us.

Her brightening eyes
served to remind
we now on spring could focus.

Then violet smiles
warmed and beguiled.
The winter nearly broke us.

She saved us all
as our hearts thawed—
beloved redeemer crocus.

Nearer

I want to breathe the open sky,
   know each star and galaxy.
I want to drink a river,
   know each brook and sea.
I want to eat of the earth,
   know each vale and peak.
I want to kiss the sun,
   know her torrid heart and be
in all these things
   nearer my God to Thee.

Walking with the Sun

Not wanting the sun to travel alone today,
I got up early and started walking west.
He yawned as he peered over my shoulder—
illuminating my way—
grinned as he shone on me from overhead—
warming my soul—
then turned and winked—
assuring me of his return—
before melting into the occidental sky.

Impending Splendor

Impending splendor.
March—a cauldron dome bulging,
ready to erupt.

Hyacinth

Dear Hyacinth, your heady bloom
is quickly filling up my room.
Although I love your fragrant charm,
I feel too much my work will harm.

Sweet Hyacinth, your blossom fair
attracts my gaze and holds it there.
Your royal purple mien is grand
but keeps me from the task at hand.

Fair Hyacinth, I must request
that you move farther from my desk.
And whether there or whether here,
I'll hold your grandeur no less dear.

Good Girls

One has trust that stands unswayed;
one desires without despair;
one, so selfless, renders aid
in answer to our prayers.

Although not known throughout the world,
perhaps you know the three.
"Why," you ask, "who are these girls?"
Faith, Hope, and Charity.

Spring Maple

She awoke with a moan
unheard by the hurried.
Corseted, upright,
smooth-limbed,
she stretches skyward,
bare arms, hands, fingers
like capillaries seeking
anastomosis with the sun.

Aware of her near nakedness,
she blushes rose red,
then dons a celadon slip,
foreshadowing the adornment
of an emerald gown
that rustles like taffeta
in summer wind.

From her raiment—
months from now,
wine-stained,
its flourishes fall-faded—
she will slowly undress,
quietly yawn,
and sleep winter away.

What My Heart Wants

What my heart wants is to beat
in the same space as yours,
at the same pace as yours,
to beat one on the other,
interlaced with yours.
What my heart wants is to be
one with yours.

Queen Azalea

Bright sovereign of the April bloom
   in luminous regalia,
no painter's palette quite compares
   to dazzling Queen Azalea.
She reigns on high o'er nigh a month
   of pastel bacchanalia,
so like a psychedelic dream . . .
   God save the Queen!
Azalea.

Sycamore

Sweet Sycamore, it's late in spring,
and you are wearing not a thing!
Pray tell me, dear, just what is this?
Are you an exhibitionist?

Your wearing nothing seems obscene
while Oak and Beech sport vernal green.
Soft red conceals coy Maple's breast.
All save you, Sycamore, are dressed.

Your comely calves and ankles bare—
as my mind sees them in the air—
I must say these and shapely thighs,
so pale and freckled, caught my eye.

My girl, now all the other trees
at least are covered by fig leaves.
You, though, aren't quite so demure,
nor are my thoughts now quite so pure.

Sweet Sycamore, let's get entwined;
I've something else now on my mind.
So let's begin the frolicking.
After all, it's late in spring.

High Spring

High spring.

The scent of wild rose swiftly
intoxicates me.

Would It Be

As lovely as the autumn valley view;
as graceful as the snowflakes' *pas de deux*;
as soothing as the warbler's springtime tune;
as fragrant as the honeysuckle's bloom;
as sweet as galas, clementines, honeydew?

Oh, would that I could share the taste
of *ae fond kiss*[1] with you.

---

1   Robert Burns, "Ae Fond Kiss," in *The Oxford Book of English Verse*, ed. Sir Arthur Thomas Quiller-Couch (Oxford: Clarendon, 1912), 571.

Unrequited

Beneath my window here each day,
like Romeo, he trills away
in search of Juliet.

I love his pluck, this steadfast wren,
but feel the pain of my small friend.
She has not answered yet.

Airborne

D-Day.
Sparrows sidestep, then
freefall into flight.

Summer: Temperance

Morning Light

The softest rays of early light
upon the cherry trees entice
and, like a slowly spreading smile,
evince anticipation.

The world awaits the fuller kiss,
the light of later morning bliss,
which, like a mother's firm embrace,
erases trepidation.

Open Range

She rolled over.
Acres opened on cool sheets.
I could roam there.

Your Eyes

Sweet, the nectar from the vine
   the world with pleasure sips.
Sweet, the honey from the hive,
   but not as sweet as your lips.

Bright, the stars and silvery moon
   amid the sapphire skies.
Bright, the sun and jonquil's bloom,
   but not as bright as your eyes.

Warm, your eyes, the guides by which
   I climb into your soul.
Warm, thereby the catalyst
   to make we halves a whole.

Lavender

What I love most about lavender,
apart from her sweet perfume:
these luminous, lighthearted creatures,
these butterflies, love her, too.

What Fool

What fool would fall
in love with you?

You are
too independent,
too strong,
too adventurous
for love to last too long.

You are
too beautiful
for your own sake.
What fool would give
his heart to you to break?

What a fool
that would be!

Ah, well, yes, uh, um . . .

that fool
would be me.

Ikey

In an ebony coat two sizes too big,
with a nose so short he snorts like a pig,
his big brown eyes stick out like a bug's.
He's one silly, shifty-eyed, sonorous pug.

With a barrel chest and a Darth Vader face,
ankles and elbows all over the place,
black all around save a warped, white goatee,
he's a pug of dubious pedigree.

Is he a dog or a bat or baboon,
the wide-mouthed creature from the black lagoon?
He eats like a bear and behaves like a thug.
He's a most voracious, pugnacious pug.

He's got a good heart, no, that he can't feign;
it just doesn't pump enough blood to his brain.
Homely and simple, oh yes, all of that,
but on the bright side, at least he's no cat!

Black-Eyed Susan

Heaven knows she has seized my soul;
my heart is forever blessed.
She stole with flaunting eyes of coal
and a sunny yellow dress.

She greets the postman on his rounds
while charming golden finches.
In scorching sun or rain that pounds,
she barely even flinches.

When dancing on the summer air,
those eyes flash in amusement.
And butterflies adorn her hair!
Oh, I love black-eyed Susan.

Learning to Say Emu

At the Barcelona Zoo,
I point and ask, "What is that?"
She says, "A me-u, Dad."

The Man in the Mirror

I stare.

This man
in the mirror
stares back
at me.

I'm wondering
if he wonders
what I'm wondering.

Am I the man
I think
he thinks
I think
I am?

He thinks I think I am.

I think I am.

I am. I am.

The Damned

Damn
these churlish chiggers
and miscreant mosquitoes,

always
burrowing and biting,
clawing and whining.

Just what purpose
do these little bastards
serve anyway?

Perhaps to prove
God exists and
has myriad messengers.

Little Brown Birds

Little brown birds,
oh, little brown birds.

Tell me if you've ever heard,
is there anything more absurd
than trying to categorize
little brown birds?

What an impossibility
to learn their danged identity.
Deprived of ornithology,
I'm driven to obscenity.
God help me find serenity
far from the russet peasantry
of each and every one of these
little brown birds!

Inward Eye

I fell awake at 3 a.m.
and could not fall asleep again.
While lying there, I turned my eyes
far inward to blue, cloudless skies,

and to a distant mountain range
that seemed familiar and yet strange,
and in that place, a glassy lake,
all still but for an eagle's shriek.

Beyond the lake on tranquil shore,
I spied a man I'd seen before.
"But who," I wondered within sight,
"is this fine man enrobed in light?"

Now drifting through that timeworn place,
my seeking eye turned to his face,
and there I saw to my surprise
my smile reflected in his eyes.

"It's you!" I cried, "How have you been?
It's been awhile, awhile, my friend.
I haven't seen you. Were you gone?"
"Oh no, I've been here all along."

A gentle hand reached out and traced
the lines of care worn in my face.
"I'm here now as I've always been,
asleep, awake, and in between."

Abruptly then, the eagle's cry,
now outward, drew my inward eye.
And looking back through waning light,
I watched the place fade from my sight.

I reached, but it was there no more.
Passing through some unseen door,
I called to him, "Can I not stay?"
He said, "You must be on your way,

but, ah, my friend, I hope you keep
peaceful dreams whene'er you sleep;
and if again awake at 3,
I hope your inward eye seeks me."

Dolly Sods

I've roamed all day unfettered,
meeting not a soul on earth.
Am I the last man in existence,
or maybe I'm the first?

In misty fields by wind-bent spruce—
a land made for the fairies—
I've drunk from streams like stormy skies
and supped on wild blueberries.

I've heard but wind and footsteps
in this second home of God's.
If Mother Nature has a name,
her name is Dolly Sods.

Gluttons

Saturated gluttons,
fat clouds squat on the ocean
unable to soar.

September

September sings a quiet song
beneath a blushing moon.
Soft as a baby's breathing,
hers is a tranquil tune.

While crickets voice a chorus
low like a muted horn,
an easy wind plays soothing strings
into the early morn.

The pastel hum of April
is a clearer song in June.
What August shouts like orange and red,
she echoes in green and blue.

September sings a quiet song,
less boisterous than July.
She sings no lusty folk songs,
just whispers lullabies.

A Summer Ending

A summer ending:
this bee paddling in my beer
grabs life's last gusto.

I Will Love You

I will love you all my livelong days,
whether held apart by walls within
or nothing more than skin.

I will love you on the day I die,
whether you fly to a distant land
or stay and hold my hand.

I will love you after heartbeat's end,
whether yours has ceased to beat before
or feels mine beat no more.

I will love you at the end of time,
whether we're a million miles apart
or still yearning heart to heart.

I will love you.

Seasons

(or The Riddle of the Tree or The Riddle of Me)

With sorrow, I sense summer ending
but relish the glory fall brings.
I'll decline with winter descending
but rise resurrected in spring!

Autumn: Courage

A Passing Breeze

The wind blows wherever it pleases.
John 3:8, Holy Bible, NIV

In my garden, a passing breeze
slowed and sought me out to tease,
   stayed long enough to muss my hair
   and stir the leaves around the stair,
then set off to where it pleased.

Lost Platoon

Hail, little grove of saplings, dead.
You soldiers to the battle led
by running water's edge were slain—
lost soldiers on a lost campaign.

Your bayonet tips leave small trace
to spot your final resting place;
their jagged peaks mark your last breath
here where, forlorn, did hope meet death.

Young soldiers, you are now all gone;
old soldiers round you soldier on.
Your gravestone stumps stand to remind
of hope and promise left behind.

No dappled light, no cooling shade
will you leave in this lonely glade;
from you no birdsongs will be sung
nor from your branches children swung.

You slimmer soldiers met the earth;
the older soldiers had more girth
sparing them their leafy branches
from the enemy's advances.

But who? This foe, where has he fled,
this one who left you grey and dead?
Your chiseled caps leave me a clue;
the killer, now I know him, too.

Mark time marching, ankles bound,
no chance to flee or go to ground.
He fell upon you fierce and fleet;
no rout could have been more complete.

He hacked and gnawed you on and on,
this ruthless, rodent Genghis Khan;
waterlogged, dismembered corpses
form this damnable ghoul's fortress.

Lodged in his macabre castle
built of boughs of faithful vassals,
he rules, triumphant overlord,
commander of a one-man horde.

Brave lost platoon of saplings, I
who did wander here now wonder why
God arrayed you here defenseless
near Lord *Castor Canadensis*.

Hirsute Riggings

Hirsute riggings of
poison ivy moor the oaks
who dream of sailing.

I Am Moved

I am moved by the touch
of your hand on my hand.
I am moved by the light
filtering through your hair.

I am moved by the solitude
of knowing in the morning,
like the sunshine,
you'll be there.

I am moved by the easy
way you love me.
I am moved by the joys
you bring to me.

I am moved by the way
that you can move me.
You uproot me,
set me free.

The Red-Tailed Hawk

She circled slowly overhead
   at least a mile from me.
It made me envious to think
   from there all she could see:

Into the regal mountain range?
   Beyond the frothing shore?
A seer of all the heavens,
   does she know all that's in store?

She drifted rather lazily
   amid the cloudless sky.
It made me rather envious
   that she, not I, should fly:

Fly off to where I have not been,
   some solitary place;
discard the weight of earthly care
   with the wind upon my face.

She floated gently, wings outspread,
   no tethers to be found.
Yet with my envy, here am I,
   eternally earthbound.

Prayer

Lord,

Help me be the man you want,
the man they think they see.
Help me be the man you need
to carry out your deeds.

Help me to deny myself
and take up after you.
Help me to continue when
I can't see my way through.

Troubadours

Two troubadours stopped here to sing.
A welcome gift of early spring—
to hear, garbed in Franciscan brown,
these minstrels of such great renown.

Fine singers, yes, and gentle souls,
their melodies sung to extol
the virtues of peace on the earth,
of lifelong love, of joy and mirth.

He took the lead, this troubadour.
She answered back, his paramour.
They circled slowly, lost in bliss,
and bobbed their heads as if to kiss.

They carried out their song and dance,
a cheerful glimpse of true romance.
Performers true, but somewhat shy,
they ached for space from spying eyes.

Impatient for their songs each day,
I tried and tried to keep away,
but moving near, not satisfied,
I startled them, and she took flight.

It caused a renaissance of pain
to hear her strike the windowpane.
Her sharply angled neck made clear,
the chanteuse I'd no longer hear.

With heavy heart, I choked and sighed
and hung my head, now teary-eyed.
I'd shown—yes, all had been undone—
the irony in loving one.

His lyric call no more returned,
he must have felt the lover spurned.
Alone and now with no recourse,
he quietly continued north.

To know this is to know my shame:
for his mute silence, I'm to blame.
I hope someday I can relieve
the suffering of one so aggrieved.

I buried her all broken, bent;
I know, if here, she would lament
upon the day I lose my love
as I mourn her, this mourning dove.

Pine Fall

Pine bark beetle kill—
a walk through the valley of
the shadow of death.

Point of No Return

A place where hope springs not at all
when nothing's left to give,
left with enough courage to die
but not enough to live;

a time of anguish wall to wall
and laboring for a breath,
when truth gets tangled up in lies,
and life now slips toward death;

living in never-ending pall,
day and night spent sleeping,
an open-mouthed and tortured cry,
but no one hears the weeping;

when paralyzed and in freefall,
alone in misery,
where in the struggle to survive,
not to be beats to be.

The Suicide

We cry for the loss of life
   and grieve for the gift refused.
We weep over deep rejection
   and the guilt of those accused.

We cry for unmade memories
   and our aid not given, too.
Even with the many years between us,
   we awake with tears for you.

The Parting Gift

We met in the doorway
that warm, sunny, fall afternoon.
I can still remember the warmth
and smoothness of your hand
as we clasped in greeting
and the roundness of your shoulders
as we briefly and awkwardly
embraced the way men do.

Just above my eye level, your bald head,
lightly polished by the sun, was shining.
We walked to the car together,
the soft creaking of crickets
the only sound accompanying our footsteps,
birds long quiet by that time of day.

As we drove off down the hill,
you said that you were sixty years old
and still concerned about
what your father thought of you.
You said it shouldn't matter,
but somehow it did.

Both of you long gone,
I now realize what you really meant
was that you didn't know
what your father thought of you.

I know that was part of the sadness
you wore in heavy-lidded eyes
and pants too loose,
betraying the weight worn off by worry.
Not long left to live, you deserved to know.

To your credit and despite your misery,
you made sure I knew the comfort
that mattered so to you,
this solace you said shouldn't matter,
but somehow it did.

While I didn't recognize it then,
you gave me the gift denied you.
Now I know, as my children know,
and I don't have to worry about it
as you did.

Maybe I'll live longer for the peace,
the parting gift of knowing
what a father's pride feels like.
And, yes, it does matter.

His New Knowledge

Emboldened by his new knowledge,
my son then lit the votive candle
for my dead father.

Appalachian Fall

Heading up in expectation,
the alluring byway beckons
as a step on Jacob's ladder,
mountain stairway to the heavens.

Sky above a blue-blood royal,
the sun emblazoned majesty
like a face encased in amber,
a gilded aristocracy.

Here below, this blazing forest
aflame in colors bright and mute.
October all around abounds
in leaves of vast, resplendent hues.

Not alone, the wind above us,
a source of rustling gaiety,
joins the sound of cheerful colors,
creating music in the trees.

Overhead, on wings conducting,
below, the trees responding more,
beats an eagle toward crescendo,
and with him now our spirits soar.

Like a Scottish hunting tartan,
an ancient Flemish drapery,
sight and sound completely woven
into musical tapestry.

The music now *adagio*
when, as we ponder our descent,
my thoughts stray off to memories
and take a melancholy bent.

Winter now is nigh upon us,
and spring potentials are far gone.
The summer breeze has left us, but
we've gold-leafed fall to cheer us on.

Looking back, a troubling surface
of seeming never-ending change,
yet beneath it lies the beauty
in how the cycle stays the same.

Like this gossamer creation
displayed before enraptured eyes,
like my climb up on this mountain,
so I must fall as I did rise.

The unwritten Copland opus,
this splendid Appalachian fall.
Aquinas's proof from motion—
the great Prime Mover moves it all.

Evensong

Calling to worship,
squirrels intone their evensong
in treetop chapels.

Your Moon

Sometimes
you are like a fairy
in constant motion
just outside my reach,
but I love the way
you stir the air, create
activity around me.
I love your soft glow,
the hum and gentleness
of your way,
the way you love
like dandelion angels
float on a breeze
or Spanish moss
drapes a tree.

Sometimes
I want to reach out and
hold you in my hand,
but I fear the sudden rush
of air might drive you away
(especially on the
wordless days).

And I miss you
when you are away.
When I see you
in my mind's eye,

it's like standing
in a doorway looking
on you in a room
as a moon might look
on its centering planet
(adoringly)
while kept at a distance
by strange, unseen,
gravitational forces.

Sometimes
I am your moon.
Always I am yours.

Clear November Day

Clear November day—
as beautiful as I wish
all my thoughts could be.

Winter: Justice

December Circus

December circus.

A cluster of moths juggles
for the waning light.

Sweet and Bitter

With freedom from want,
would I recognize treasure?
Without knowing pain,
could I comprehend pleasure?

With freedom from failure,
would I taste success?
With no threat of illness,
could I feel at my best?

Without seeing black,
would I understand white?
With no view of darkness,
well, what then is light?

With freedom from risk,
would I savor reward?
If never unloved,
could I sense I'm adored?

With freedom from fear,
would I know if I'm brave?
When everyone's youthful,
where's the wisdom of age?

Without any valleys,
well, where then the heights?
With no fear of death,
is there value to life?

A life without contrast
is less than a whole.
Without sweet *and* bitter,
we'd have half a soul.

Knowing Virtue

Prudence,
   knowing when to go;
Temperance,
   when to stop;
Courage,
   guts to wield the sword;
Justice,
   strength to not.

Tormented

"Come out, come out,
you need fresh air,"
whispered the winsome wrens.
"Come out, come out.
There's freedom here.
Come outside with your friends."

"Come out, come out,"
the finches fussed,
"and do it now. Don't tarry.
Come out, come out.
Just look at us.
We've neither want nor worry."

"Come out, come out.
You need a break,"
the sweet nuthatches nudged.
"Come out, come out.
Make your escape.
Think upside down like us."

"Come out, come out."
I'll send my heart;
my body must remain.
"Come out, come out."
I'm begging you,
please end your sore refrain.

"Come out, come out."
It hurts to be
reminded of the cost.
"Come out, come out."
My liberty,
you see, is what I've lost.

"Come out, come out."
They mock my name
outside these prison walls.
"Come out, come out."
For crime and shame,
I threw away it all.

Quiet

Sleeping babies,
woods at night.
The ocean depths,
morning light.

A spotted fawn,
a dog on a lap.
A soaring bird,
a cat at nap.

Angry lovers,
the wind in trees.
Distant mountains,
the softest breeze.

A sense of calm,
a sense of place.
A soul at peace
din would erase.

A gentle touch,
a loving look.
A wink, a nod,
fish in a brook.

Falling stars,
first kisses.
Aged lovers,
near misses.

Praying hands,
the gentle womb.
A walk on sand,
the tomb.

Dachau

Visiting Dachau,
my son asks, "Daddy, where are
all the animals?"

The Paradox of Time

Once upon time did I wait
to catch sight of its measured gait.
I stared, but it moved not at all.
A day, it seemed, could scarcely crawl.

To coax a day by force of will
made it stand completely still.
Even an hour appeared to balk
when I dared that hour to walk.

Then I saw, the less I gazed,
the more the movement of the days.
When I learned to have some fun,
the days somehow began to run.

With my mind on timeless things,
the weeks unfolded hidden wings.
Even months had learned to fly
when I no longer cared to spy.

Winter, spring, summer, and fall
hardly notice me at all.
Years that once moved at glacial pace
sprint now as if in a race.

Tally horses in a pen,
or let them loose and run with them?
Preserve the dike and all it saves,
or let it break and surf the waves?

Hesitate and count your days,
or boldly lead them on their way?
Bittersweet and yet sublime
is the paradox of time.

Love Worn

Dagger love, the passions led,
quick to cut, we quick to bleed,
serves us now our daily bread,
servicing a better need.

Puzzle love, the pieces wedges
forced together firm and tight,
simpler and with ragged edges,
clings now no less through the night.

Sharp-eyed love, the crystal vision
quick to spot and to object,
blurred now and with less precision,
kinder and less circumspect.

Flaming love (Do you remember?),
quick to flare and quick to harm,
burns now as a bed of embers,
smoldering but no less warm.

Perfect love in all its splendor,
like the golden band in round.
Love worn gentle, soft, and tender,
wiser but no less profound.

Winter Solstice

My heart quickens as my languid lover stirs.
Beneath sheets of billowed snow, she wakes
and peeks at me with a sleepy golden eye.

Feverishly, we embrace, and I drink kisses
of warm honey deep into my soul.
We live and briefly glow in amber glory
until she again forsakes me for slumber.

And I am left awake
to ache for my narcoleptic leman.

Cornucopia

God gives us food and plenty
   and ample draughts of wine.
He gives us good companions
   but only so much time.

We share with joy and laughter—
   create fond memories—
a feast of hours and places
   with friends and family.

We taste with smiling faces
   the fruit of field and vine
with no regrets thereafter
   and small regard for time.

Then suddenly it's over,
   the horn of plenty gone.
A friend has left the table,
   and the clock is ticking on.

We're saddened by the empty cup,
   the plate now whisked away,
but cherish our lost friendships
   and prize our finite days.

Grace

She from pieces makes a whole
while untying knots in souls.

The unworthy are embraced.
Know Him and you know her face.

Forever and Enduring

Like the fields of grass or flowers
   waving to and fro,
I know I flourish but an hour
   before my time to go.
Yet, for this man with numbered days,
   the truth is reassuring:
God's love will not wear away;
   it's forever and enduring.

February

The earth in deepest slumber grows
   restless under ice and snow.
Windswept, frozen, silent, numb,
   she dreams of what with spring will come:

When by the great, mysterious hand,
   dark gives way to light again,
and fire once more burns in her hearth
   to warm her face, her hands, her heart;

when landscapes dull and brown and mean
   ignite in shades of pink and green,
and birds—returned in wingèd throngs—
   explode with reassuring songs;

when all, it seems, escapes from death,
   reanimates and regains breath,
and Flora, Fauna, and Ostara
   celebrate dear Primavera.

But as for now, she must dream on,
   sleep through her journey 'round the sun,
await the sunlight angle change,
   and rendezvous where prearranged.

So, Gaia, dream; there is no choice
   but to wait for resurrection's voice
to sound the sweet, primeval cry:
   Awake! Awake! Awake! Arise!

Epilogue

To All Ye Lads and Lasses

I've heard that *ale's the stuff to drink,*
for fellows whom it hurts to think.[1]
As for me, I say it's true
that ale's a drink for thinkers, too.

You can throw the wine glass out
and draw me a lager or a stout.
Please, no Chablis or Chardonnay.
Pour me a Guinness or Chimay.

Yes, when I've something I must cheer,
no wine for me, man, make mine beer.
And fill it 'til it's overflowin'.
Keep these rosy cheeks a'glowin'.

And on the day when I am dead,
you can cork your white and red.
Just tap into a cask of ale,
and lift your glass on high "To Dale."

And now my tale I will suspend
in toast to you, my dearest friends.
So here's to all ye lads and lasses
who prefer what's in beer glasses.

---

1   A.E. Houseman, "Terence, This Is Stupid Stuff," in *A Shropshire Lad* (London: K. Paul, Trench, Treubner, 1896), 95.

About the Author

Husband, father, grandfather, brother, son, friend, biologist, veterinarian, pathologist, and former Army officer, Dale has been writing verse off and on since he was sixteen years old. While he wrote most of the poems in this collection within the last dozen years, one of them he wrote at age nineteen—can you spot it? Dale believes that, like our Creator, we humans delight in creating. He hopes his family and friends will find some inspiration in this book to begin or continue to explore their own imaginative expressions in whatever medium suits them. He also hopes that, as he did, they will find their own delight in doing so.

www.ingramcontent.com/pod-product-compliance
Lightning Source LLC
Chambersburg PA
CBHW031928090426
42811CB00002B/118